Woosh, Things Up A Bit:

The Principles of Perception Management™

Dedication

I dedicate this book to my three sons: Jaron, Jordan, and Joshua.

For my youngest son, Jaron:
Since the day he was born, I knew he was a different type of human being. He already had the Woosh factor. I have always had an overwhelming feeling that he will do great things. As I watched him grow up (he is now 21 years old at this point), I saw that he had proven my feelings correct. His attitude and instincts are such that he may have the highest level of innate emotional intelligence of anyone I have ever known. And he is an awesome musician, to boot!

Yes, I am a proud papa, but more than that, I truly believe I am blessed that the Universe saw fit to allow me to be his parent. I learn so much from him. He is the one who actually said I needed to write this type of book back when he was about 14!

I just want to say, Jaron, I love you with all my heart, and I would not be where I am today if I were not your father. Having you in my life has helped me overcome so many of my personal demons. For that, I will be eternally grateful. I can't wait to hear what music you and your brothers will create and the amazing other things you will do as you continue on your journey to adulthood!

For my middle son Jordan:
He is arguably the warmest, most kind person I know. He has an amazing talent for making people feel really comfortable around him. This is so special. Speaking of talent, he is such an incredibly gifted

musician, songwriter, and performer. For over 10 years now, I have been in awe of his musical abilities. I am absolutely certain that he will perform and share his music with millions of people all over the world. I know he and his brothers will create amazing music that connects to people!

There are so many ways you have helped me personally through the past several years, Jordan. Your ability to forgive and love seems unending. I don't know how I would have made it through some of my serious challenges without you in my corner. For that, I will be eternally grateful.

Jordan, I also love you with all my heart, and I am incredibly grateful to get to be your dad! I can't imagine a life without you (and your wife) in it! I cannot wait to see what music you will continue to bring to the world. I love you forever, no matter what!

For my oldest son Joshua:
He is my creative, critical thinker. He has always looked at things with a solid, critical eye and a sense of wonder. He wants to know how things work, how people think, and what influences everything. He always wants to solve problems and learn the "how to" stuff on his own (trying to follow included instructions for things was always a challenge - he always found a better way). He also has incredible insight into many subject areas because he loves learning and constantly tries to understand all sides of any situation or challenge! He is also a gifted musician (even though he doesn't really believe it).

As with his brothers, I believe I would not have been able to conquer so many of my fears (Skydiving, just to name one) and inner demons. Your love and support (and sometimes direct scolding and calling me out on BS) have helped save me…really! I want to be a better person because of you, buddy.

You have such a wonderful combination of "free spirit," "adventure seeker," "entrepreneur," and "purpose-driven" that you have become an incredible young man and natural leader! I know more great things are in your future. And like your brothers, I love your creative side and the music you write. I know you and your brothers will share incredible music with the world! I love and respect you so much, Joshua.

Preface

Having been in marketing for over three decades. I actually arrived late to the game to utilize LinkedIn for anything other than a glorified resume. I really started to utilize LinkedIn for the first time from a real business standpoint in early 2024. As a result, through connecting, expanding, and developing my network, I learned there was a real interest from people to understand the principles of Perception Management™. Making Perception Management understandable to people has been challenging because of all the "marketing jargon" and catchphrases and confusing directions.

This is where Woosh comes in. A simple word that brings everything together to fully understand what perception management really is.

After publishing numerous articles and videos and giving multiple presentations on the subject, a User's Guide emerged. Encouraged (or should I say "pushed") by my youngest son to write it "now" vs. waiting, I embarked on the development journey! And well, here we are.

Introduction

My goal for this User's Guide is to help raise awareness of and understanding what Woosh is and the Principles of Perception Management™. I truly believe that everything we do in life, both personally and professionally, is influenced by the perceptions we have (and the perceptions others have of us).

By understanding how to Woosh and recognize internal and external perceptions, we can learn how to modify them. This will lead us to maximize who we are, why we are, and what type of mark we want to leave on this world. From a professional standpoint, by understanding and implementing "Woosh," we can best provide our customers and clients with exactly what they need and want in a sustainable way. Further, we create the value we believe in ourselves.

You see when you "Woosh," you change perceptions, and you change what's possible. My hope is that this guide will help you get there!

Contents

Chapter 1
Understanding What Perception Actually Is.

We have to start somewhere, so let's start with me trying to explain what perception actually is and how it affects what we think and feel. Although this is an interesting topic to me, to some, this first chapter may be a little slow - but it is an important foundation for the other chapters. I promise things get really interesting as you continue reading!

According to a great paper by Fiske & Taylor, published in 1991, Perception is the process of selecting, organizing, and interpreting information. This process includes the perception of selected stimuli that pass through our perceptual filters, are organized into our existing structures and patterns, and are then interpreted based on previous experiences. Although perception is a largely cognitive and psychological process, how we perceive the people and objects around us affects our communication. We respond differently to an object or person we perceive favorably than to something we find unfavorable.

But how do we filter through the mass amounts of incoming information, organize it, and make meaning from what makes it through our perceptual filters and into our social realities?

According to Fiske, we take in information through all five of our senses, but our perceptual field (the world around us) includes so many stimuli and information that our brains can't process and make sense of it all. So, as information comes in through our senses, various factors influence what actually continues on through the perception process."

That was a mouthful! Basically, what they are saying is simply this:

EVERYTHING we see, hear, touch, smell, etc., affects how we perceive anything and everything. Fiske goes on to identify the steps we all apparently take to process all these stimuli and information.

- **Selecting:** This is the first part of the perception process, in which we focus our attention on certain incoming sensory information. Think about how, out of all the possible stimuli you pay attention to, you could hear a familiar voice in the hallway, see a shirt you want to buy from across the store or smell something cooking in a restaurant as you pass by. Apparently, we all quickly sift through and push away all kinds of sights, smells, sounds, etc. The question is, how do we decide what we focus on? We most often pay attention to the information we find most relevant to ourselves. Or, as Fiske & Taylor say, "we pay attention to information that is salient to us."

What the heck does "salient" even really mean? The dictionary defines it as "the degree to which something attracts our attention in a particular context." What attracts our attention can be stable or abstract.

For example, a person's religion may become salient around a specific holiday like Christmas or Easter. Or if you are out on a hike, are really hot, and hear a waterfall. That is sure to be salient to you. Although this can differ from person to person, I have found that one's degree of salience is usually based on visual things, stuff we hear, or simply things we are interested in. Another thing that affects what can be salient to us is what we expect something to be.

Honestly, seeing or hearing things isn't always a positive thing. For example, you are at a concert, and there is a couple next to you that won't stop singing at the top of their lungs (you can't hear the group you came to see). Or the car next to you with the stereo turned up so loud that you can feel it vibrating your body. Lots of stimuli can grab our attention in either productive or distracting ways. Learning how to minimize distractions when we have something critical to say is a skill worth learning. Hopefully, you will pick up some tips as you continue reading the other chapters in this book.

We have all probably heard through our high school or college speech courses that altering the tone or volume of our voice can keep people's attention. Another way to keep people's attention is through gestures and body language. The best way to keep people's attention and be "salient" to them is through the content we communicate. People tend to listen to content that either meets their needs or sparks emotions. This is why storytelling in marketing is so very important. It directly shapes people's perceptions about a product, service, company, event, speaker, etc.

- In a paper published by Coren et al. in 1980, he defined the second part of the perception process as **"organizing."** Basically, we categorize all the information we receive based on our current behavior patterns. We evaluate everything based on proximity, similarity, and difference. However, for me, this doesn't go far enough. I also believe that we sort things based on familiarity as well. Just because something may be new to us doesn't mean it gets our attention.

For example, how often have we stood in a line waiting to get served at a restaurant, and the host or hostess assumes that if we are standing near another set of people, we must be all together? Two steps further apart, this perception will not happen.

As Coren said, we also group things together based on similarity. For example, I am a tennis player. I was out with a friend (who does not play tennis) and was dressed in tennis clothes as I had a match later in the day. We were at a restaurant for lunch, and our server asked my friend how long we had been playing tennis together. My friend was dressed normally, but he assumed he played tennis with me because we were together. Or if you see three guys together with athletic builds, dark hair, and glasses, you might think they are brothers.

We often organize information based on differences as well. This means we may assume that someone who looks or behaves differently from the rest of a group doesn't belong with the group. Here, you want to be extra careful because perceptual errors that involve people can be really awkward, hurtful, or even offensive.

- Lastly, we come to the third part of perception, called **"interpretation."** When we select and organize our incoming stimuli and information, this happens very quickly and sometimes without conscious thought. However, interpreting everything is often a much more deliberate (and conscious) step in perception. This is actually where we assign meaning to an experience. We rely on all our past experiences like a giant database of the mind.

Obviously, our internal database affects our behavior. Here is an example: remember a time when you had to do a group project in high school or college? You perceived one of your group members as really shy because they were super quiet. You came to this perception based on how you have interacted with shy people in the past. As a result, you may incorrectly assume they would not be good at presenting. And in reality, they are brilliant presenters, and our perception was wrong.

A great saying from Steven Covey, the amazing author of 7 Habits of Highly Effective People, goes something like this: "when someone walks into a room, you can think they are smart, charming, and competent. Or you may think they are a pompous ass who is full of themselves. When they first open their mouth, they prove which perception is right." Again, we draw from all our experiences and immediately start to perceive someone to be one way or another based on what we see. And it gets solidified when we add what we hear to our internal database.

So, what are the important takeaways from all this?

- Perception is the process of selecting, organizing, and interpreting information.
- Given the massive amounts of stimuli we take in, we only select a portion of this information to try and organize and interpret. We select information based on what is relevant to us based on what we first see and hear.
- We tend to organize information based on proximity, similarity, difference, and familiarity.

- We interpret information using our life experiences, which are our internal database; we basically assign our perceptions based on all our accumulated knowledge up to that point in time.

Coren, S., "Principles of Perceptual Organization and Spatial Distortion: The Gestalt Illusions," *Journal of Experimental Psychology: Human Perception and Performance* 6, no. 3 (1980): 404–12.

Fiske, S. T., and Shelley E. Taylor, *Social Cognition,* 2nd ed. (New York, NY: McGraw Hill, 1991).

Chapter 2
Woosh - This Crazy Thing I Call Perception Management.

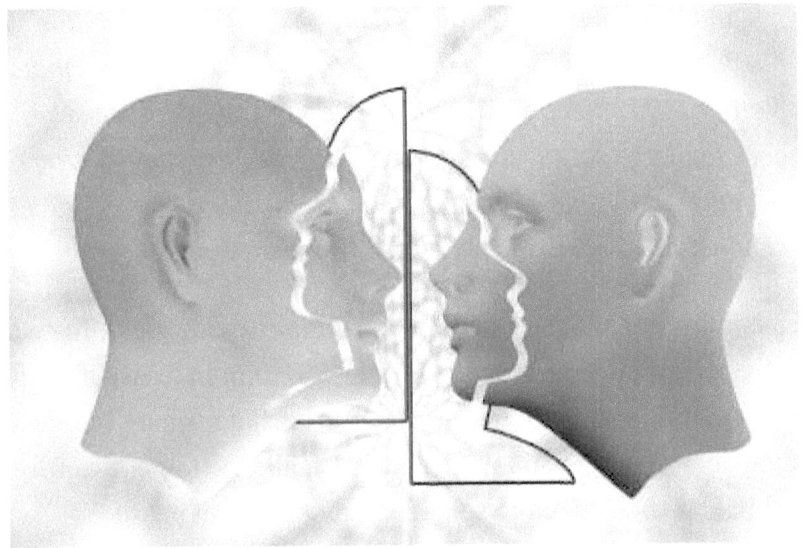

Perception Management has been around for as long as there has been civilization! Only people didn't know what they were really doing. Leaders would gain their "followers" by presenting information as they understood things at the time, and their audiences would perceive them in their own way.

If people perceived someone to have great strength (aka Sampson from the Bible), they believed the leader could do great things. Or perhaps the great philosophers who espoused their version of "why" the world was the way it was. Readers, again, develop their perception, and it becomes their own reality.

Perception Management was finally officially "coined" as a real thing back in the early days of the U.S. military of all organizations, around the time of WWI. In fact, when you Google the term, the first thing that pops up is The Department of Defense definition. As you read the definition, it may give you the creeps. It certainly did for me!

> *"Actions to convey and/or deny selected information and indicators to foreign audiences to influence their emotions, motives, and objective reasoning as well as to intelligence systems and leaders at all to influence official estimates, ultimately resulting in foreign behaviors and official actions favorable to the originator's objectives." (Webster Dictionary)*

Sounds a bit devious and manipulative, don't you think? In today's society, perception management is quite different in terms of business and marketing strategy. It certainly is not some clandestine, manipulative way to communicate to an audience to get them fooled into thinking and/or feeling something that may not be true!

However, not unlike the military's definition, it does combine what is known as "truth projection" and "psychological intent." I define this as "how you want to be perceived" = truth projection...." why you want to be perceived a certain way" = psychological intent. Am I beginning to sound like I am spouting a bunch of psychobabble? This is certainly not my intent! In a later chapter, we will discuss understanding the "who" and the "why" behind all your Woosh, and you will have a strong understanding of the importance of both psychological intent and truth projection.

As I take you on a journey to understanding Woosh and the principles of Perception Management, I feel it is important to clear the air first. For years, business strategy and marketing firms have focused on "positioning" products and services and "hooking" their clients by using a bunch of industry buzzwords such as brand image, value propositions, buyer personas, value chains, and for those of you digitally savvy; second pages and lots of other "marketing speak."

And let's not forget these overused fun marketing phrases: brand essence, brand identity, brand voice, brand persona, TOPOF (top of the funnel), BOF (bottom of the funnel), and so on and so forth. The reality of this is that none of these "how you position" tactical approaches matter if you don't first master the "what" you are positioning and the "why" you are positioning incredibly well. This means you have to fully understand the market and the perceptions of the market where you want to compete.

Contrary to conventional belief, this doesn't come down to branding, your "brand essence, " value messaging, etc. This is all marketing mumbo jumbo. Yes, an excellent marketing person developed every one of these descriptive terms and concepts to sell people something.

Perception management, what I call "Woosh," is a strategic approach that tries hard not to subscribe to the buzzwords to "hook" you as a customer. Rather, this approach coaches, trains, and develops you and your teams to focus on modifying market perceptions so that you can consistently grow your business by doing the right things at the right time for your customers over and over. What's great about implementing the principles of Perception Management is that once you master the "Wooshing," it is easily repeatable and a lot of fun to do!

So, let's get started! Let's break things down by revisiting the meaning of the word Perception. In the previous chapter, I gave you a very deep dive into what the word perception means at the granular level and how people arrive at a perception. Here, I want to simplify it and make it easier to understand.

In my world of business and marketing, perception is simply what people "think or feel" about a product, service, company, person, and so on. As shown in the previous chapter, people get their perceptions from various stimuli. However, in marketing, perceptions are almost always based on what we see and hear directly about the subject. This can be through written information (articles and online content), visual imagery (e.g., TV commercials), or what they may hear (radio, podcasts, etc.).

It might surprise you to learn that most perceptions people have are usually wrong. They are not what the person, product, or company ever intended.

Here is an example of internal misperceptions within a company: how many times have you gone into an update meeting? You know, the type of meeting where each department provides leadership with a status update of their respective areas. As you listen, you begin to think about your part of the presentation, and you inevitably stop listening to the other folks providing updates. You perceive yours as important and don't want to mess up your chance to present. However, in doing so, by tuning out the other folks, you miss the opportunity to see where and how people perceive themselves within the organization. This can dramatically affect what you do in your department. But you didn't pay attention, so you don't know.

This may sound minor, but because of your perception internally, you may be letting your colleagues down (and of course, several folks are doing the exact same thing as you, so it turns out that except for the senior leadership, no one paid much attention during the meeting). What a large waste of everyone's time!

What I am talking about begins with getting super clear on who you are internally and within your department. Interestingly enough, I was working on a client engagement, and my team quickly learned that many employees didn't actually understand what their company really stood for and why they developed and sold specific products in the areas they did. Of course, they had seen the CEO's corporate presentations about their "mission" and "vision," 5-year plans, and so on. But the reality of their situation was this: all that information from upper management was about as clear as a puddle of mud to them.

If your employees are ambiguous about why the company exists (other than to make money), imagine what your customers in your markets may perceive. It gets you thinking, doesn't it? This can be very eye-opening and a great learning exercise! This whole perception thing is complex – but it doesn't have to be hard to understand.

Folks, you have to be super clear on WHO you are as a person, company (or a product or service). Then, you have to be equally clear on WHY you are who you are. Understand exactly why you are going after a particular market with specific products and services. Further, you can't just focus on the value you "think" your product or service may bring, but rather, what influence will you have on the market as a result of a perceived value? The key to everything is how exactly you want a given market to perceive you as a company. It all starts there! Every strategic plan should begin with "who," "why," and "what" before you move onto "how."

This is where Wooshing things up a bit comes into play. By helping you get laser-focused on who you are, what you have to offer, and why you want to offer it in the first place, and leveraging this understanding, The principles of Perception Management, when implemented correctly, help mold the "how you want to be perceived" in the marketplace and then help you not only achieve your desired perception but also maintain it. This is what gains new customers, keeps your existing ones, and grows your overall profitability.

In its purest form, woosh (perception management) is actually the act by which someone thinks or feels about your product or service. In other words, interrupts perception! Directly after this interruption is your greatest opportunity to position yourself, your company, products, and services. Doing this effectively will build the foundation of how you will be perceived in your market. Getting to this result should be an eye-opening journey that is unique, fun, and, most importantly, sustainable!

Chapter 3
How Perception Management Can Affect All Our Lives.

Perception Management plays an integral role if you look around at almost everything you see, read, or hear. As I mentioned in the last chapter, what we perceive to be true often isn't. What we think others perceive is often mistaken. Thanks to an amazing network connection via LinkedIn, I was introduced to a fairy tale that illustrates Perception Management very well.

This fable by John Godfrey Saxe (who lived from 1816 to 1997) illustrates how many people can be around the same thing but perceive it differently.

Once upon a time, there lived six blind men in a village. One day, the villagers told them, "Hey, there is an elephant in the village today."

They had no idea what an elephant was. They decided, "Even though we would not be able to see it, let us go and feel it anyway." All of them went where the elephant was. Everyone of them touched the elephant.

"Hey, the elephant is a pillar," said the first man who touched his leg. "Oh, no! It is like a rope," said the second man who touched the tail. "Oh, no! It is like a thick tree branch," said the third man who touched the elephant's trunk. "It is like a big hand fan," said the fourth man who touched the ear of the elephant. "It is like a huge wall," said the fifth man who touched the belly of the elephant. "It is like a solid pipe," said the sixth man who touched the elephant's tusk.

They began arguing about the elephant, and they all insisted he was right. It looked like they were getting agitated. A wise man was passing by, and he saw this. He stopped and asked them, "What is the matter?" They said, "We cannot agree on what the elephant is like." Each one of them told what he thought the elephant was like. The wise man calmly explained to them, "All of you are right. Every one of you is telling it differently because each of you touched a different part of the elephant. So, actually, the elephant has all those features that you all said." "Oh!" everyone said. There was no more fight. They felt happy that they were all right.

From my perspective, the moral of this story is that there may be some truth to what someone says (or perceives). However, one person's truth is often different from another's because he perceives the situation, person, product, market, etc., differently. How do you decide who is right when they all are?! How do you Woosh things up a bit?

With Perception Management (what I call Woosh), people, businesses, products, or services need to be very clear about the desired outcome they want (how you want to be perceived by others). This is classic marketing and/or personal branding and/or PR at its finest moment. The moment when you do the actions necessary (branding, positioning, imagery, etc.) is to ensure your target audience - whoever that may be - perceives you, a product, a service, and your company how you intended. This is what Woosh is all about!

Woosh is a science and art form combined. My team sees many people and companies completely unaware of how this affects new customer acquisition and existing customer retention. So many missed opportunities!

People and companies who do this well often are at the top of their markets, have more social media followers, have their music listened to more, sell more products/services, and so on. When you master the principles of Perception Management and you Woosh things up a bit, there is nothing you can't achieve.

Here is another really great example. Which perception is the right one?

Artist Unknown

DAYDREAM STATE: As we go through another day in the office, we can look around and see people sitting at their desks, working away on their projects. Walking through the halls, we pass conference rooms where we can see people engaged in spirited discussions and planning meetings. We notice the artwork or posters on the walls that show "who" our company is.

We think to ourselves how we completely understand exactly our role in the company, why the company exists, its culture, its values, and its goals. We are excited because everyone seems to be on the same page, and senior leadership continually communicates effectively and often about all the key areas we need to understand.

Um, NOPE! This doesn't sound like anyone I know. How about you?

The reality is that we often have no idea what is going on with our colleagues in those conference rooms and, sometimes, even in our own meetings. Why? Because leadership has been focused on earnings and ROI and has done a less-than-stellar job of solid communication around exactly "who" the company is and "why" they do what they do (products or services).

Wouldn't it be amazing if you knew exactly what each area in the company does and why? Further, it is equally amazing to fully understand what your company is about, your senior leadership's passion for making things happen, and your actual value to the company.

One of my hopes for writing this guide is that it can help you understand the importance of Wooshing things up a bit in the workplace. Perception management is important to ensure your company's employees, products, and services are perceived as you desire in your market space. However, unless or until everyone within your company is quite literally on the same page with respect to "who you are" and "why you do what you do," it won't matter how you position your company's products or services in the world. More often than not, your target customers won't really understand who you are and why you do what you do in the long term. Your business could lose sustainability.

You will hear a lot of marketing agencies or management consulting companies call this "Branding your company." But folks, it is way more than that simple marketing jargon! It has to be your company's way of life. People will try to tell you a brand has its own persona or personality.

It all sounds a bit elementary, doesn't it? Well, that is because it actually is! However, this concept of internal perception seems to be something quite new to many companies. I am constantly dumbfounded by the lack of knowledge of senior leaders and entrepreneurs in this area, which is unfortunate. Companies that do well with Woosh tend to become market leaders. I have worked in organizations where, for years, senior leadership would hold monthly or quarterly "status" update meetings with their senior and middle managers. Then, the information is "trickled" down to the rest of the organization.

I have seen where Regional Sales Directors are brought in for these types of meetings and left confused about why they were even there. These meetings often end up simply being "information dumps" and marching order assignments for the next month or quarter. Do I sound familiar with situations you can relate to? Maybe you have found your company guilty of doing similar things. What a waste of everyone's valuable time and intellectual resources. Also, what a huge miss on the perception within the organization!

Wooshing things up a bit can help senior leadership deal with being on the same page (across the board) regarding how you want to be perceived internally and externally (not just personally, but your respective roles and the company itself). This can be a very fun and dynamic endeavor and should be "gut-checked" every quarter to ensure consistency of thought and message. To begin with, leaders must first get super clear on "who they are." Why does the company actually exist, and why are you selling what you sell? And most importantly, how do you want the company, products/services to be perceived by your employees? Remember, employees provide a lot of free positioning for your company out in the market. I think you want them to get this perception right!

A very important tool to use to ensure everyone (employees, managers, and senior leadership) is on the same page is to do some type of a 360 review. This ensures all internal perceptions are where you want them to be and where they need to be to ensure your company's success. I have had many experiences where I learned that employees and their own managers were far apart in their perceptions. This almost always leads to employees becoming very unhappy in their jobs. And possibly worse, managers build a case to manage employees out of the company without allowing opportunities to modify perceptions. Does this sound familiar to you? It happened to me a couple of times during the past 30 years, trust me!

NOTE: Woosh Marketing Consultants, LLC helps companies get super clear on how to Woosh things up a bit - implement the Principles of Perception Management and then work with them to develop the appropriate strategies to achieve desired outcomes. We have a fun, fast-paced workshop that ideates everything from a company's values (not value propositions) through manufacturing processes. Everything combined equals your employees' perception and, ultimately, your marketplace will have. We call this Perceptual Mapping.

Chapter 4
You Don't Know, What You Don't Know.

I have always found it most interesting that many people are touting their "wisdom" and throwing around that word because it is so mainstream. In reality, wisdom is the actual use of and experience from doing something and learning from it. It is the actual "lessons learned" that bring wisdom. Lots of people have experienced things but learned nothing. In fact, many people do the same thing repeatedly without learning from it and expect a different result (we probably have all heard that this is one of the definitions of being crazy).

I often get questions from potential clients about my experience (or lack of) in a specific market or business area. For example, I did a project in the Aerospace industry not too long ago. Interestingly, I am neither a physicist nor a calculus numbers guy, nor do I even understand the study of properties moving air and the interaction between air and solid bodies moving through it. I think that is aerodynamic speaking.

In fact, before this project, I didn't really know much about airplanes, rockets, or anything related to the industry. So, how could I possibly bring value to a team working on new product development?

Well, what did I know? I knew a lot about overall business strategies, and, most importantly, I knew a lot about how to whip things up and implement the principles of Perception Management. Wooshing is similar across all industries. The principles are exactly the same. The "how" to get it done tactically may be different. The process is often the same as developing the tactics.

The project was to position a new type of proprietary manufacturing process for aerospace extrusion products. They faced a lot of competition but had a significant (and legitimate) advantage in manufacturing their products vs. everyone else in the market. Unfortunately for them, they had muddied the waters in the market with multiple "value propositions" imagery that tried to explain their manufacturing process. Nothing was clear at all about what made them unique and why someone should care.

A traditional "marketing agency" steered them down the road of storytelling and then developed multiple assets to simultaneously put out into their marketplace across all media platforms and even a large trade show. With only their actual process logo looking the same for each asset, customers were not clear on the messages or the stories they were telling (because there were several different ones) or their value and advantages. In fact, they were no longer clear about the product and service.

I have had several clients who previously worked with a traditional marketing or advertising agency but didn't get the results they desired long-term –after spending tens of thousands of dollars and lots of time and effort. Not getting the desired results can be frustrating and make you distrust your instincts or marketing agencies.

Here is a strong example: "You don't know what you don't know." This company didn't know that buzzwords and telling multiple stories for a singular product may actually confuse their customers. What do I mean? Over the years, I have found that a clear process works well to ensure success.

Classic marketing agencies and consulting firms will continually use the same approach with every one of their clients, from using the same outlines for marketing plans to the same templates for social media posts to even the exact same music on video content (just because it is trendy). They also get bogged down in providing clients with marketing buzzwords like "branding," "brand essence," "value propositions," Story-telling, and similar. This is all fancy speak for positioning who you are and what you have. Most of today's marketing agencies and ad agencies seem to put the cart before the horse - so to speak. They focus on the "how" something should be promoted before helping companies get clear on the "who," the "what," and the "why."

You shouldn't try to position a product, service, or even your overall company until you are clear on a few things. Companies must first clearly define "who" they are, "what" they have, and "why" they want to produce it in the first place. Why be in business?

Too often, companies will hire a marketing agency or advertising firm. They have their "go-to-market" strategies in hand, but they leave out multiple parts that are necessary to be successful because they simply don't know what is really needed in today's 15-second attention span theater we call the internet. And digital marketing is way more than SEO and SEM.

When completed, all their assets looked amazing, their text/copy seemed exceptional, everyone was excited to launch this campaign that their marketing agency developed, and then the campaign did "ok" for a while, and then…….crickets….they didn't get the result they desired.

The sales team was confused about which selling tool to use and when, and the manufacturing folks were confused about the "label" given to the manufacturing process to "brand" it. No one was on the same page. They continued down the road of "not knowing." I bet you can guess where I am going with this.

Internally, they didn't nail down (and effectively communicate to all employees their "Who, What, and Why"). They were unclear about how they wanted to be perceived internally or externally. Folks didn't know this perception would be the catalyst to drive sales and profitability. They really needed to Woosh things up a bit!

The very first thing my firm tells our clients in a breakthrough meeting (some may call it a discovery meeting) is that Perception Management internally and externally in your marketplace is key. Unless or until everyone is on the same page, sustainability can be a real challenge. Also, we help instill that this is a continual process, not a one-time event. At the very least, 2-times a year. Companies need to always keep Woosh at the forefront of their minds!

As I said, without knowing anything about the aerospace industry before I started this large new project, we helped an aerospace extrusion company to ideate exactly who they are, what they really do, and why they exist to do it.

From there, we ensured every employee (down to the maintenance people) clearly understood these values. We spotlighted their desired outcome – how they wanted to be perceived in their market. We worked with their internal graphics team (there was no need for an outside ad agency) to develop specific assets that would position their products exactly how they wanted to be perceived.

Remember, Wooshing is an ongoing process, not a one-time event. A few weeks after the launch of their new campaign, my folks executed message testing for a group of their target audience and, based on the feedback, helped them implement a few perception tweaks. I am proud to say that a little over three years later, this company is a market leader in specialty extrusion for the aerospace industry.

Chapter 5
The Clarity of the "Who" in You.

First things first! With any good business or marketing strategy, you must be clear about who you are! What do I mean exactly? Let's say you are ready to launch a new product or service into a relatively crowded market. You did all necessary due diligence and properly identified a market problem or opportunity. You have all the specifications for the new widget you want to create to meet this market objective. And you realize that the "know-how" is not currently in your company's knowledge base. In other words, it isn't "who" you are as a company today.

This doesn't mean you can't gain the required knowledge or, through an acquisition, buy the knowledge needed to develop the product; it just means that today, it isn't who you are. So, you are now at a crossroads.

Folks, you will see this repeated throughout this book: you must be super clear on "who" you are and what you can do right now (not necessarily in the future)! And you have to decide if this is how you want to remain.

For example, my firm did a really interesting project with a plastics manufacturer. It was another type of plastic extrusion company (like the aerospace example I shared previously). They were incredibly innovative with the types of products they could make using their own custom-made, proprietary extrusion machines. In fact, they were the only company in the world that could do specific specifications for customers. No other company could even come close. Their reputation was impeccable. They were perceived as the "can do anything" extrusion company. What a great perception, right?

However, they were actually not a "jack of all trades" when it came to all areas of extrusion. In fact, there was one specific area where they were much weaker than competitors. This market area was a commoditized market with a dozen competitors actively seeking to undercut one another. The result was a less-than-awesome product mix but super low prices to the market. Customers were being sold on this product as being "good enough" and easily replaceable, so they almost always went for the cheapest price.

However, our client had never put out any products that were considered just "good enough." They only put out exceptional, high-quality products and did not want to lower their manufacturing standards. And to me, that was super impressive. However, this one market area was worth over $1 billion, and they sold less than $150K annually of their own product into this market. You can imagine how attractive it was to simply put something out there for sale, even if it was considered "cheap," just so they could grow their market share.

Ultimately, my firm did an exercise to help them clearly understand the "who" they are and "why." We started with a full portfolio analysis of their entire product mix. We reviewed all manufacturing procedures, the types of workers on the manufacturing floors, which they had in packaging and shipping, and so on. We reviewed their sales organization and marketing teams. When we were fully finished with our review and had collected all the data, we did what is known as an internal perception analysis. All part of Wooshing things up a bit.

We researched how their employees viewed working for the company. What they each perceived was the value the company offered to customers and what the corporate vision/mission was. We spoke with customers to learn how the company was perceived (products, employees, management, etc.). When we completed this exercise, we gathered all the information and presented it to senior management.

We learned this: The company uses only the best, highest quality materials. It hires only the most skilled workers with significant experience in the industry. Customers recognized their sales and marketing teams as being the strongest in the industry overall, and the overarching perception was that management was ethical and fair and provided great value and service to customers.

The employees perceived themselves as an asset to the company and believed their work mattered. In other words, this company had a very strong culture of respect and recognition. Further, it had one of the lowest turnover rates of any company I have ever worked with in my 30 years as a professional.

So, what does this all mean, and how does it relate to the "who" a company is? Well, in this particular case, the conclusion was simple. This firm should not move into this market area unless it can create change. Their other products and services are not commoditized. Since they have never competed on price, the perception would have changed dramatically regarding the type of organization they are today!

Walking away from an "easy," cheap entry into a $1 Billion market area isn't easy. But these decisions become much easier once you are clear on the "who" you are in your industry.

Our client consciously decided to keep to a higher standard and not lower their value to customers by compromising either production or materials quality. Instead, they decided to put their efforts into researching a better way.

They focused on developing a new kind of product that would have a superior function, require less replacement, and have a fair cost. They used the same approach to market entry that has always worked for them. They could keep their current perceptions steady, and the result was the development of a brand new, disruptive product that changed how customers felt about "good enough" in this market area.

In fact, they effectively positioned themselves to customers as "not having to settle for good enough." Although their costs were higher compared to others, their value was significantly greater, and they provided cost-effectiveness over time. Within a little over a year post-launch, our client effectively interrupted how customers thought about this market and the available products and grew to be the market share leader.

They got super clear on the "who" they are and "why" they do what they do – specifically, they were clear on how they wanted to be perceived.

What can you do personally or professionally right now to ensure you are clear on the "who" you are and want to be?

The next chapter will provide a set of exercises you can do that I think may provide an eye-opening experience!

Chapter 6
Perceptual Mapping: A Brief, 3-Step "How to" guide.

In his book "Seven Habits of Highly Effective People," Steven Covey writes, "Seek first to understand, then be understood." In essence, to achieve our personal or professional goals in life or business, we must begin by understanding who we are, what we do, and why we do it exactly. The following steps can help you map out a clear understanding of these areas and identify opportunities for growth and change.

STEP ONE: Understand exactly who you are right now!

- Write down who you think you really are: What you produce, what your strengths and weaknesses are (be brutally honest with yourself), things you love to do, and how you believe others see you (how you think you are perceived).

- Go ask others! Ask them what they think about YOU. We should all do a 360° multiple times in our careers. Now, do one of your perceptions yourself! Tell people to be super honest (and there are ways to keep this anonymous as well so people will be more willing to help). Ask them what they perceive about what you say you love to do and the type of person you really are. For your business, ask your customers these questions.

- Using all the data you have collected (personally and from your outside friends or customers), you can map out a comparison chart of what you believe vs. what others perceive. Look at any areas of disconnect and GET EXCITED!

Huh? Why get excited? Because this is an opportunity for growth, either personally or professionally. You now have a clear view of the perceptions you need to modify. This way, the "who" you really are perceived exactly as you want by others.

STEP TWO: Understand your "why."

- Now that you have all the data on who you are and how others perceive you, you need to be super clear on the motivation or the "why" behind what you believe and what others perceive.

- Be sure to write down the exact reasons why you believe some things (e.g., why you think you have a particular strength or weakness, why you love doing x vs. y, and so on).

- Additionally, be sure you understand the "why" behind what others perceive. Understanding exactly why they think something about you is important to help develop the right strategy to modify any misperceptions others may have of you (or a product, service, or company).

STEP THREE: Determine "what" you want and your desired outcome!

- Unfortunately, this is an area where we all need the most help. Too often, I find that most people and companies focus on the "what" they want to achieve before they get clear on the "who" and "why" they are currently. To map out what you want to achieve, you must first master steps one and two.
- Let's now assume you are super clear on knowing who you are. You now know how you are perceived (or how your products/services are perceived). And lastly, you know why you believe as you do and why others perceive you a certain way. With this information, you can clearly map out exactly what you want!
- Using all the information you have obtained, write out exactly what you want to achieve.
- Write out all the reasons why you want to achieve these things – be honest and clear.
- Write out exactly how you want to be perceived (either personally or professionally). Write out how you want these perceived and why for products or services.

Now comes a very important part:

- Once you have these things written down, make a vision board. Design your board (either electronically, in an app, or the good old-fashioned poster board with pics). Visually display exactly what you want to achieve. Trust me, you can find an image for literally anything and everything – just look on Google!

- After you complete your vision board, make a recording. Capture everything orally that you want to achieve. Make sure it matches up with your vision board. I find it best to simply tell a story about your vision.

A really good marketing strategy will include an exercise called "war games" or strategy ideation. That is exactly what this really is: a foundation for ensuring you are (and remain) clear on your target goals.

So, let's get a little focused on companies and products. How can you effectively design and launch a new product or service in a market area? How can you be sure it will be perceived how you want and have sustainable sales?

In the next chapter, I will provide solid information to get you there!

Chapter 7
PERCEPTUAL PLACEMENT: 4 Areas to Effectively Achieve Your Desired Perception For a New Product or Service.

When an established company discovers a true new market need and develops a product or service that can meet this need (and is first to market), this can quite literally shape the future of your entire company, not just with the promise of a potentially new growth engine for the organization but also with how the company will be perceived in the marketplace.

How you launch this product or service will dictate how the market sees you—as unique, innovative, visionary, responsive, or even as "manipulative" (if perceived as forcing it down their throats without a genuine need). This perception may influence how you launch all future products and learn/discover market needs. So, the key is to get it right (or as close to right as possible).

It all starts with Perception Management. When you were discovering and/or identifying this new market need, how did you do it? If you reviewed all the available published data, conducted primary research with a core group of existing customers and prospective customers, developed product scenarios, and tested those as well, then you were certainly traveling down the right path... But that isn't enough anymore. That is too old school. In today's 15-second attention span theater, you must elevate this process significantly.

There are 4 key areas for ensuring your new product or service launch hits the desired target results.

UNDERSTAND INTERNAL PERCEPTIONS:
- Learn exactly how your company is perceived by its employees (what they believe about your culture, vision, leadership, and all products and services).
- Why is this important? Whether you are a company of 5 or 2,000 people, every employee is a walking/talking piece of marketing collateral. If employees strongly understand "who you are" and "why you exist," they are much happier in their roles and will speak positively to others about the company, products, and services. It is super important that everyone is on the same page here.

UNDERSTAND CURRENT EXTERNAL PERCEPTIONS:
- Take the appropriate time (and spend of resources) to learn exactly how your company, products, and services are currently

perceived in your market areas. This is vital and serves as an excellent baseline for growth.

- If you already have a perception counter to what you are trying to achieve as a company, then you have a possible uphill battle when it comes to launching new products.

Here is a real-life example: my firm was engaged with a client who wanted us to completely revamp their marketing. This company was historically seen as "old school" – great quality, solid product mix, but lacking exciting innovation in how their products looked or were packaged for consumers. They had no disruptive technology either.

We learned that not only distributors of their products believed this perception but also actual consumers who used their products. They held this same belief for years.

You can imagine my team's challenge when we helped them develop a completely new and innovative line of products, convincing the market that this company had "changed" its way of thinking around product development without compromising quality.

CREATE A PERCEPTUAL MAP FOR PRODUCT DEVELOPMENT:

- Internally, decide how you want the products or services you launch to be perceived in the market. No, this isn't as simple as creating a "value proposition" and go-to-market strategy. Again, times have changed, and to be successful, you must evolve along with them.
- You need to clearly define exactly how you want to be perceived and then map out an exact process for getting there. This requires a few strategic steps:

- If you already have a clear market opportunity, develop a product or service that meets this need and repeatedly test the specs through primary market research. Be sure you cover every area that could be "misperceived." Ask questions about the look, feel, performance, and packaging (colors, textures…literally everything). This serves as your baseline for moving forward and tweaking as needed.

- Develop messaging based on all the data inputs you learn so that you can be perceived in the best and closest way possible to your goal and desired outcome. Then, develop the right type of collateral to communicate this messaging (and again, do your research and learn how folks like to be communicated with. Involve your sales teams since they are the front line. Ask them what tools work best for them). The super key here is consistency of message, look, feel, and frequency.

- Message testing follow-up – at 60 days, test your messaging and ensure that what you want to be perceived is, in fact, being understood that way. Tweak as necessary to be sure you remain on track. Do this again at 120 days and then at the 180-day mark post-launch. Properly ensure a strong recall for your message and that you have the right communication out in the market for how you want to be perceived. I am always stunned that very few companies do this step well or at all.

PERCEPTION MANAGEMENT – RINSE AND REPEAT:

- Once you achieve the desired adoption for your product or service, you should conduct quarterly spot checks on how things are perceived.

- Make appropriate tweaks to maintain the desired perception. It's also a good idea to conduct these checks internally, either quarterly or semi-annually.
- Ensuring that your employees and your market are consistently aligned enhances your credibility. Moreover, your employees gain additional pride in working for a company that communicates effectively.

Folks, these steps are dynamic and follow a proven methodology that has worked for literally hundreds of products and services my firm has been involved with. It works whether you are developing something completely new and are first to market or if you are essentially a "me too" type of product.

Chapter 8
Perception Management & Micro-Targeting.

Recently, I had the pleasure of reading an excellent article and watching a detailed video on the importance of microtargeting in today's digital marketing age. Specifically, how can microtargeting help you reach specific customers in unusual market areas (e.g., a specific neighborhood in a state or a country like India or Singapore etc.)?

This article aims to help you understand how Perception Management can strengthen your microtargeting efforts! First, let's be clear on our definition of microtargeting: for this, I will borrow from the article I read (special thanks for sharing it with me, Esha Panda)

Esha, a LinkedIn "top influencer" for her country (India), really defines this well. Microtargeting is a way to create customer segments based on definite demographic and psychographic patterns. This makes it easier for content marketers to target individual consumer segments and sell useful products to the relevant buyers. Though widely treated as content marketing jargon, microtargeting is a really simple concept.

You need a focused customer behavior analysis (strategy) to identify and categorize their buying patterns. Unlike the common perceptions of mass outreach, microtargeting helps you reach out to your potential prospects and ensures a better conversion. – Esha Panda, India
Ok, so now, with a focus on microtargeting, where does Perception Management fit in? The following are 3 important things to consider when microtargeting when the emphasis is on Perception Management:

- Absolutely, positively understand your micro-target audience. How? Do perceptual research to learn how these targets perceive a product or service (yours or your competitors). Knowing this information will be essential in developing the right approach to market to them.
- Using the information of how these targets currently perceive products and services, clearly define exactly how YOU want your products or services to be perceived by these targets. Be super clear on your desired outcome.
- Once you are master #1 and #2, this is when the fun begins! Using your newfound knowledge of your target market and exactly how you want to be perceived, you craft a 2-pronged strategy to reach your target audience.

- First, based on your new insights into how current products or services are perceived (and how you "want" to be perceived), ideate on the best messaging that will resonate with your targets about what your solutions are.
- Second, ideate how you will interrupt the way your targets feel and think about the product or service they currently use (there are many ways to interrupt folks – want to learn some cool ideas? Reach out to me, and we can strategize together).

Now, execute your interruption and positioning strategy! Because this is laser-focused on a set of micro-target audiences, you have a much better opportunity to provide exactly the kind of product or service these folks seek. In my experience, microtargeting is essential – especially in today's information age, where there are so many choices and a variety of available globally. You have a much smaller audience with microtargeting, but your conversion rate is nearly 50% in most cases. Meanwhile, with marketing to the masses (which is what DTC folks commonly do), you often achieve conversion rates under 5%. This means you must spend much more time, effort, and financial resources to achieve the same result as microtargeting marketing.

I don't know about you, but I will take 50 qualified adoptions out of 100 vs. 50 out of 1000 every day of the week – it costs a lot less money, and the results are often much more meaningful. And the best part is this is scalable to multiple micro-target audiences worldwide. The power of multiplication vs. duplication works every time.

Chapter 9
Knowledge is not power. We all have been taught Wrong.

Folks, I had the most amazing experience speaking with one of the principal Experience Managers at a company that pairs professionals with mentors. The company was called Everwise. They specialize in putting business professionals together with mentors who can help them grow their soft skills.

During this discussion, we were having a dialogue around knowledge and the fact that often, many people know exactly what they "can do," "should do," or "need to do" in a given situation but don't take the action needed to implement or execute and leverage the knowledge they have.

We all know the expression, "Knowledge is power." In reality, this saying is 100% WRONG. Why do I say this? First, anyone and everyone can learn something. We can all gain knowledge of the "how," but if we don't take any action to use this knowledge, then learning it is a wasted effort. You see, it is in the execution or implementation of learned knowledge that power is really found.

My colleague at Everwise coined a quote that I completely relate with: "Knowledge without application is simply information." These words are so true. Say this sentence again in your head right now. Feel the meaning. For years, Tony Robbins, the performance guru, has said, *"Knowledge is not power. Knowledge is only potential power. Action is power."*

Now, let me add my two cents worth as it relates to perception management: What we see, hear, touch, smell, taste, and ultimately understand (in essence, everything that provides us with knowledge) dramatically affects our perceptions of the world around us. By simply absorbing what we learn without the "application" part, we cannot modify our personal perceptions and ultimately change any outcomes.

What do I mean exactly? Take a small business, for example, and the company learned that a huge market problem had been identified through market research. Further, many customers are experiencing the same issue/need, so they have a large target audience. This company knows it has the internal capabilities to develop a product that offers a great solution to this problem. However, they get bogged down in the "how" before they get clear on the "What" and "Why." As a result, they take no action to move forward with developing this product and leave the market open to competitors to swoop in.

Believe it or not, I have clients who really are thinking like this. The reasons vary: it is too hard to manufacture (perceived barrier to entry), it is too expensive to market to our customers (perceived barrier to entry), it will take too long to distribute (perceived barrier to entry), and so on. They have a long list of perceptions that shape their company's beliefs. These perceptions of their situation become excuses for not doing something vs. a motivating reason to find a way to bring a product or service to market.

People who have read my articles know that I preach far and wide that Perception Management is a science and an art combined to empower individuals and companies to reach their desired outcomes. However, to do this, they must be open to thinking about their situations differently. Most importantly, they must be open to taking action and applying what they learn from their customers, markets, and employees.

What do I mean by thinking differently? I mean changing perceptions. If you perceive something to be true, it becomes your reality. So, modify your perception. For example, if a manufacturing cost is currently too high, you will perceive it as a barrier to entry. So, this should spark your motivation to find a way to manufacture at a lower cost. Guess what? As Tony Robbins always says: "there is always a way if you are committed." Meaning you can always lower your costs without cutting quality. Just because you don't know the way today doesn't mean you can't find a way tomorrow!

The reality of life is this: if you can manage your perceptions, you change what's possible. Knowledge isn't where the power lies; using and leveraging your knowledge is the most powerful thing you can do.

And Perception Management provides the pathway (tools and skills) to your best implementation.

Chapter 10
The art of real, actionable market research.

Here is a question for you. Have you ever taken a survey? Something similar to: on a scale of 1-10, with 1 being "never likely" and 10 being "most likely," will you recommend our service to a friend? Have you ever wondered what someone can do with information actually learned from all the answers in between ("somewhat likely," "maybe likely," "likely," "not likely," and so on and so on)? Each one of these answers provides a different data point.

I bet every one of us has probably taken a survey like this and perhaps recently. Almost every company we do business with sends out customer surveys to gain information that can help them improve their service, product, and a handful of other areas. This is a GOOD thing.

Unfortunately, most companies and people go about this in the wrong way.

In fact, over the past 30 years, I have found that this type of survey most often does not yield any truly actionable information. Marketers and business leaders have been conditioned by marketing firms and consulting companies to do these research projects for years. However, unlike personality tests that ask similar questions in a variety of different ways, in today's 15-second, digital attention span theater, questionnaires like this aren't answered thoughtfully, and people often rush through them.

There are studies about these surveys that suggest that if people are satisfied but not excited, they will often give a 7, as this seems like a good neutral score. Additionally, if they are really happy, they will often give an 8. Very few folks actually give 9s and 10s because they think there is always room for improvement. Often, the numbers don't tell the real story or certainly not a complete story.

Interesting information about the "5-star" rating system is also available. If people are genuinely happy, they will most often give a 4 (again, they always believe there is room for improvement) unless completely blown away by customer service. I was shocked to learn that many times, if you see 1000s of "5-star ratings" and after digging, you won't find many 3s or 4s, it likely has been skewed results (by design). How is this done? I learned about a growing "cottage industry." Companies can actually hire firms that do surveys about your products or services. However, these firms never actually use the product or service. Their employees complete surveys repeatedly, representing different personas and/or demographics. These people are provided a set of instructions to follow – this is most often done to combat negative feedback received by people or to build a quick following for a new market entrant. Who would have thought about this right??

As you can imagine, from a perception management standpoint, I hate these services and these types of surveys. Again, even when conducted well and ethically, they don't yield enough actionable information for real business or marketing planning. The best surveys I have seen (and used) do real primary research that is more of an art form combining quantitative with qualitative.

For example:

Keep things simple – give people only 3 choices: How would you rate this product (Good, Fair, or Poor)? Follow each quantifiable question with one that requires some type of written comment. Example: Why did you rate this the way you did? Instead of an open-ended "What would you change?" or "What did you like best" question, get super specific. Use something from your products' positioning to call out for information. Say your product is more comfortable to use vs. competitors; the question could be: "What specifically did you like most about the comfort of our product?"

Using a combination of these simple choices followed immediately by a written direct question will almost always yield actionable information that is both qualitative and quantitative from the same set of responders. My team often uses this type of research in Perception studies to learn specifics about how a product or service is perceived and why. There are many ways to obtain this type of research – my personal favorite is "in person" live events at tradeshows, focus groups, or places where your product and service is sold. If executed correctly, online research can also be quite effective.

I recently worked with a company that did an annual satisfaction measurement survey for their overall company (they did one internally with employees and one externally for their customers). Hundreds were completed in both areas. The average internal score was 7.4 out of 10. Externally, it was an 8.3 out of 10. Last year's survey had 7.5 and 8.1, respectively. What actionable information was achieved? There was no statistical difference, and internally, the company was still showing a lower level of satisfaction vs. externally. This means nothing was done with the information from last year because it wasn't actionable. A whole year wasted!!

Chapter 11
The Key To Almost All Communication.

Have you ever had a personality test done? Or if in a business setting, the "communication type" personality test? The big ones are the DiSC or Meyer's Briggs. They are designed to help you understand the best ways to communicate with other people by providing insight into their personality types. Over the years, I have found them very useful – but only when I have significant time to learn all I can about every person I interact with.

Unfortunately, in today's world, most of the time, it isn't possible to do a personality review on the scale necessary to master how you modify your communication style for every individual you may interact with professionally (or even personally).

So, what can you do in meetings to ensure a positive outcome regarding your communication style? It begins with using Perception Management techniques.

For me, I believe you must master the "30-second size up." I have found the best way to read the room (and this is just one dude's opinion) is to be the last one to speak, if possible. If you are a "member" of the meeting, this shows all other participants that you wanted to seek first to understand, then be understood (aka Steven Covey's 4th habit). It also gives you great insight into others based on how quickly, often, and loud or soft they communicate. Further, by not speaking, you are observing. I have learned that you can size up a person within 30 seconds and determine the best way to effectively communicate with them on the spot.

If you lead the meeting, your lack of immediate speaking shows attendees that you fully want them engaged and care about their input. In today's short-term attention span theater, we often get too bogged down focusing on "what" we communicate and sometimes forget about the "how" we communicate.

Personally, I strive to keep things simple. Empathetic communication is key, and to me, reading a room is much more important than understanding all the different personality types. Further, sometimes you have that "1-2 minute" meeting in an elevator or a hallway, and you don't have time to assess anyone (no one is that good, haha) for more than a few seconds. Therefore, always approaching from a position of empathy to me is the way to go.

Easier said than done! How can you do this effectively in only a few seconds? It is all in observation: observe immediate body language, tone of voice, where their eyes are directed, and lastly, how quickly they respond on their end of the discussion (immediate responses without much thought often are a "tell" that someone isn't truly interested in what you are communicating).

What's great about exercising this "size up" muscle is that, over time, you will get really good at it. I have found it to be every bit as effective as the larger personality/communication tests that are given to help do the same thing!

Chapter 12
The Perception Principle.

Have you ever discovered a bad product or service, yet it seems to be growing in dramatic multiples, and you cannot understand how or why? I think we all have. There isn't one easy answer, but I challenge you to think about this: could it be because the company that provides the product or service (which you "perceive" to be bad) has actually done an exceptional job of positioning its perception out in their market space?

The Perception Principle is simply this: companies that do well with seemingly "bad" products or services do so because they define exactly how their audiences want to be perceived. Inevitably, a few of us perceive the product/service poorly. In reality, though, these companies have found a way to be perceived as having an amazing product or service...or maybe amazing follow-up and follow through....or incredible customer service.

These companies got laser-focused on "who they are" and "why they exist." Then, they worked hard to be perceived as they desired for their outcome. This means they worked on their internal perception with their employees (down to the manufacturing level). With everyone aligned with how the company wants to be perceived, they clearly found it easier to position themselves in their respective marketplace and achieve the perception they wanted from customers.

They say that perceptions are >95% of someone's reality. To me, that screams **WE NEED TO MANAGE OUR PERCEPTIONS!**

Chapter 13
Outcome is the "What." Don't worry so much about the "HOW."

Have you ever wondered what happens when you get things "right?" When all your planning actually works flawlessly, and nothing gets out of play or goes astray. Every piece of the puzzle fits together perfectly, and you wonder how you got so lucky that absolutely nothing went wrong.

Me either! Why? Because that is life, folks. Too many people focus on "how" to get where they want to be vs. the actual reason behind "why" they want to be there. It really isn't about stressing on the how, but rather how you REACT to the things that don't go the way you planned, wanted, intended, etc., and you still get the desired outcome you wanted.

Approach everything with your desired outcome in mind. Once that is super clear, you can work on finding ways to achieve it. But you need to be prepared to accept that how you achieve your desired outcome is almost never what you expected, and that is ok!! Focus on the things you can control and choose to be in the moment. It is this behavior that shapes the perception others will have of you (personally and/or professionally). Really, that is what success and growth are all about.

Don't mistake this as not planning. It just means you have to understand what you are planning before you begin the actual act of planning. Too many companies focus on building products or developing services and then trying to find a way to fit them into an existing market or, worse, trying to create a market that does not yet exist. In marketing, mumbo jumbo speak is often referred to as "building a faster horse" or "prettier widget" or one I am sure you are all familiar with; "putting lipstick on a pig." I am guessing you and your company do NOT want to be perceived as any of these things.

Chapter 14
Are you POOR or RICH (Hint: it has nothing to do with money)?

You can learn how to change how you think about *anything* and *everything!* Sometimes, you have to take common phrases with everyday meanings and SHAKE things up! I hope that in the next few paragraphs, I succeed. I want to change the way we all think about being poor or being rich!

The famous Zig Ziglar has a great way of looking at entrepreneurs. In fact, he coined the phrase "wantrepreneur" long before you heard guys like Mark Cuban use this label on the popular TV show Shark Tank. Ziglar looked at wantrepreneurs as a bucket of people who "pass on opportunities regularly" or **POOR** and compared them to people who seized any and every opportunity each time they came along. He spoke a lot about his definition of luck : "preparation + opportunity = luck.

To me, this is a great foundation, but in today's age of the 15-second attention span of theater and all the stimuli we all face in our lives, this definition doesn't go far enough anymore.

I love Ziglar's **POOR** acronym but want to contrast it with something different. In a recent video, I presented what I call a "Perception Maker Moment" (or PMM for short) on what I perceive as the difference between being a positive person and having a positive mindset. I also wrote an article on the same subject. I want to take things way further than a positive mindset for this guide. I want to discuss having a **RICH** mindset.

So, let's first break down what Ziglar was talking about when he says wantrepreneurs are **POOR** (pass on opportunities regularly). This often means the person wasn't prepared to take some type of action. Either they were scared or thought it was too hard or would require too much work or didn't have enough time, and on and on.

Again, I refer to the great Tony Robbins. He always says people like this have what he calls an "I should do it mindset." And as we probably all know, life is full of people who always say, "I would have," "I could have," and, of course, "I should have." From personal experience, I know we don't hear enough people say, "I did!"

What happens is these people let so many great opportunities come into their lives and quickly leave without taking any real action to seize them and take advantage. As Robbins goes on to further say, unless or until you get a "must do mindset," you will be stuck with "I should have," and simply (as he says), you will "should all over yourself, time and time again!"

Well, I hate people "shoulding" all over themselves, and I am here to help! I want to help you create a **RICH** mindset and end your "shoulding" once and for all! That is why I created this special acronym.

Let's keep things simple and start with your basics: What do you mean you need to be **RICH**? It has nothing to do with money or accumulating valuable things in your life. In fact, it really is specifically about perception management and exercising your emotional intelligence muscles.

I created a simple acronym to help illustrate this:

    R = raise (decision to take action)
    I = intensity (focus)
    C = Challenge (Interrupt/disrupt)
    H = History (how you have been thinking or feeling)

RAISE your INTENSITY to CHALLENGE your HISTORY. Ok, so you must be scratching your head now, right? What the heck is this guy talking about??!!

Simply put, you have to implement the principles of Perception Management and get into the RICH mindset.

First, you must decide that you need to make a change. Just this decision alone will begin to **RAISE** your level of thinking, and your intensity and excitement start to rise. Many people get to this stage and falter. How awful is it to know you want or need to make a change but never really do anything about it? The answer to getting you to actually take some action is this: you must get super clear on the change you want to make – do NOT yet worry about the "how" you will make it. In past articles, you may have seen me discuss the importance of being super clear on "who" and "why" you are before worrying about the "how."

Focus your **INTENSITY** on this clarity.

Ok, ya'll (yes, I live in the deep south – Georgia), you are getting some nice momentum going! With your newfound super clarity and your intensity kick into high gear, you must now CHALLENGE how you have been thinking and feeling about things historically. You must modify your perceptions! (We are moving from "should do" to "must do" here)

You must look at how you have always perceived things (your **HISTORY** of perceiving situations, events, products, services – you name it). By challenging your history, you actually *"interrupt"* or *"disrupt"* the way you think and feel about people, products, services, or anything else in your world.

Once you have successfully interrupted this thought process, you can modify your perceptions and achieve your desired outcomes. You will have achieved a **RICH** mindset! What's even more great about this achievement is that as you practice this newly acquired skill, it gets easier and easier to have this mindset automatically. And even better, share and teach others!

Chapter 15
Pat on the Break! 3 steps to undo your "mind-crowding."

In life, as in business, things get hectic. I don't just mean just everyday business of what we may be doing. Rather, the hectic pace of our incredibly busy thought processes. Throughout our day, week, or month, we all have our minds going at 100 miles per hour. And with all the external stimuli available today, it isn't just around the holidays that we get into this state.

We wake up "thinking" about everything we need to get done today, later in the week, by the end of the month. We are thinking about work, family, health, money, and dozens of other things.

This isn't necessarily a bad thing …BUT… our problem is that we think about all these things **AT THE SAME TIME!**

I was once a Product Director at a Biopharmaceutical company a few years ago. I was in charge of their ADHD medicine franchise. Yes, this disorder is real, and I had the opportunity to see it firsthand through a series of ethnographic research projects that helped me better understand what people (and not just kids) go through that have it. I have even co-authored a children's book with the great Dr. Bonita Blazer (a noted expert in childhood ADHD). The title of this book is "How Do I Feel." It is based on 100s of actual patient interviews with children between the ages of 6-12.

In our discussions with these amazing kids, we saw a common theme they all shared (we also found this with adults). It became clear how we could describe to general people what these patients go through on a daily basis. I was super excited because we were able to help parents understand how medication + therapy can provide the support and behavior modification they were seeking, but more importantly, it can help these kids have normal, productive engagements with other kids and in their classes.

So, what does any of this have to do with you? Well, I was literally lying in bed the other night and started "mind-crowding" with too many thoughts. I also found myself unable to get comfortable lying in any particular position. And suddenly, I was reminded of the way these kids with ADHD explained how they feel every minute of every day!

Let me explain it this way: imagine you are sitting at your desk at work. No matter how you sit, you are just a bit uncomfortable, so you shift your position (you do this repeatedly, *never stopping* shifting positions because you can never get comfortable). All the while, as you are uncomfortable sitting, you are thinking about your bills that are due, the Christmas shopping (or Hannukah) you need to finish, the client project that you need to start, your son's/daughter's upcoming recital, how much you hate going to Walmart for anything, how will you grow your business, you need to go to the bank, what you are having for dinner, and on and on and on.

I am betting each of you is shaking your head in agreement! Can you relate? Is this perhaps happening to you **RIGHT NOW??!!**

I am NOT saying you have ADHD! But I am saying this: we all can have a temporary ADHD-type physical and mental condition. It is when we allow **"mind-crowding"** to creep into our day. Stress hormones release, we can't get comfortable where we are sitting, and now we allow "worry" to rent too much time from our lives.

We can all get like this several times during the year, especially around the holidays (and one of my friends is also planning an extravagant wedding for his only daughter <u>right now, and</u> his "mind-crowding" is peaking at the moment).

We may not be able to completely shut our minds down to this type of thinking 100% of the time, but we certainly can make a HUGE difference by implementing one of the principles of Perception Management. I call this principal *Interruption*. Interrupting how you think or feel about the stimuli in your life right now can allow you to dramatically lower your stress.

Here are the 3 steps to doing just that:

STEP 1: INTERRUPT

Pat is on a mental break! Acknowledge you feel overwhelmed, stand up, take a short walk, and say (literally) out loud: I don't want to feel like this anymore! Yes, go try it. It actually works! This is a strong interruption. Why? Because you have physically spoken out loud, so you personally must pay attention, you have stopped your thought process almost completely – at least temporarily.

STEP 2: REPLACE

Now that you have literally interrupted your thinking and feelings replace your thoughts with something you really love. For me, I have a "go-to" action. That is MUSIC…After interrupting how I think or feel, I listen to one of my favorite songs! For those of you who were able to see my recent video on this same subject, you learned that my go-to song at the moment is "Sing a Song" by Earth, Wind, and Fire. I am telling you, folks, you cannot even *remotely* feel down or stressed listening to this song (LOUDLY, of course)! This go-to action allows your mind to "pat on the mental breaks." You can't go back to everything you were thinking about simultaneously. It's not going to happen – honest!

STEP 3: GET CLEAR

You interrupted your thinking and feeling, replacing it with a "pat on the mental break" action. Now, you need to avoid going back to that previous mental state. The very best way I know how to do this is by **GETTING CLEAR** on your immediate priorities. I personally like to do things in "3's." Everything can't be a priority. So, write down your top 3 "must-do" things. Not the stuff you "should do" (in a previous video and subsequent article, I spoke about Tony Robbins saying, "People keep shoulding all over themselves). If you are diligent and you absolutely get these 3 things done, something incredible happens. Literally, all the other "stuff" doesn't seem so stressful anymore. It is this awesome chain reaction!

You have consciously decided what is most important, and your brain finds a way to get those 3 things done. All this equals a lower stress and anxiety level.

I don't want to mislead you into thinking this is easy. **WAIT....it is!** But Dave, if this is so easy, why isn't everyone doing it??!!

Understanding what needs to be done is always the easiest part, but the hard part is accepting that this behavior takes practice. Like any other skill you learn, the **Principles of Perception Management** take time to master. I know I may have to do a "pat on the mental break" 5 separate times before it actually sticks. But that is ok! Each time I modify my perceptions, I lower my stress or "freak-out" level further and further.

You may experience this in business when you have multiple projects with varying timelines, and everything is happening ALL **ONCE!** When I used to manage large marketing teams, I would observe people's behavior on a regular basis. When I started to see the theme of chaos come around, I knew the entire team needed to "pat on their mental breaks." You can do these 3 steps alone or as a group. You will get the same awesome results!

Chapter 16
The Art Of Being Selfish. It Is All About Perception Management.

Growing up, we likely heard *"Don't be selfish"* from our parents. Or you need to *"share"* more. *"Don't just think about yourself."* I am sure we all can relate to this one way or another. And this is relevant across all cultures.

Let me ask you all a question: When you do something nice for someone else, how do you feel? When you share something with another person, how do you feel? When you donate your time or financial resources (if you are able) to charity, how do you feel?

I am betting you all are telling yourself that I feel really good when doing any of those things. Am I right? We can't deny that doing something considered "selfless" feels good!

So here is the dilemma: Why do we really do nice things for others? I know you probably say it is because these are the right things to do. Or, because it is what makes us human…or something similar. The reality is simple: we really do things for other people because it makes us feel good! And guess what? Feeling good is actually **selfish**!

That bears repeating: We do things for other people because it makes us feel good! Yes, it may be the "right thing to do," but *NO ONE* does something for another if it doesn't make them feel good. Even when you "sacrifice" something you love dearly so another person can be happy – that, too, makes us feel good!

This means we really do these types of things for OURSELVES! And that, my friends, makes us all a little bit selfish! We do things nice things because they make us feel good – because they make us feel passion or inspiration…but make no mistake, we do nice things because *WE* want to *FEEL* good! I am here to tell you that this is absolutely, positively, **100% ok!** The conventional (meaning old) definition of selfishness simply is not correct!

In my "Atti-tune-up" seminar, I will speak about the "winning effect." This is the "feeling" you get from winning a contest, sporting event, etc. Or the feeling you get when you have crushed it in a presentation, project, or something that was important to you. It is the exact same feeling you also get when you do something nice for someone else. It is **supposed** to feel good! The Universe set it up that way!

This is a key difference that separates us from all other animals. This is actually part of our sophisticated ability to have free will.

If it didn't feel good doing something kind for another person, guess what? We likely wouldn't do it (unless, of course, we are a Saint – and that is the only exception). The Universe has a distinct vibration that draws all living human beings together. This vibration is something everyone can know and relate to…the vibration of "feeling good."

The Law of Attraction states: If you "feel good," you "attract good" back into your life. I always add when you feel good, you **"DO"** good things in your life. It can be an amazing cycle of awesomeness! You get to feel good all the time and do things that are of value to other people. Yet again, this is the epitome of being a little **SELFISH**!

The dictionary defines selfish as:

"Concerned exclusively with oneself: seeking or concentrating on one's own advantage, pleasure, or well-being without regard for others."

I want to **DISRUPT** this definition because although, on the surface, it is correct, the part about *"without regard for others"* simply isn't true in every situation. And there is nothing wrong with feeling good about yourself.

One of the key principles of Perception Management is the fact that we all do things based on our perceptions. I am guessing, growing up, we all believed the word "selfish" was something that was bad, and you wanted to avoid this type of behavior at all costs. Our parents ingrained it into our core.

I challenge this (especially in today's society). I submit that not *all* selfish behavior is bad. There are actually "good" types of selfishness. These types compel you to do something kind for another because they make **YOU** feel good! I further submit that if you perceive that it is *"ok"* to feel good when you do something for someone else and allow yourself to own this little piece of selfishness, you will do a **LOT** more things for others. Again, this is a great cycle of awesomeness!

Look at the definition of philanthropy:
"The desire to promote the welfare of others, expressed especially by the generous donation of money or one's time to good causes."
I would add: ***Because it makes us feel good!***

I am sure a few of you either nod your head in agreement or shake your head and want to bash my head about now. So here is my challenge to YOU:

Think of one time when you did something kind for someone else. Think about how you **FELT** knowing you helped another person. Remember how that affected the rest of your day.

Now tell me you **DIDN'T** feel good! So, if you felt good, what was the real reason you did the "good deed?" We all have the desired outcomes we want to achieve. ***FEELING GOOD*** is one of them.

Life and business are all about **#Perception Management**. Getting clear on how YOU perceive the things in your life and, equally important, how others perceive you (or in business, how you perceive your own products/services and markets and how your customers perceive you) is absolutely vital.

Those who can **INTERRUPT** the way they think and feel (their perceptions) about themselves, a product/service, or a company and then modify these perceptions to achieve the desired outcome will be the happiest, most successful folks around. So, interrupt how you think about the word "selfish."

Chapter 17
The Art of Influence vs. Manipulation - 3 Powerful Steps to Help Your Business Thrive.

In today's business world, grabbing potential customer's attention is becoming increasingly more difficult. There are so many stimuli across many different media platforms that it is very hard to "grab" someone's attention while remaining ethical and authentic.

You not only have to have a clear and concise (and focused) brand message, but you also must have an authentic, consistent image as well. Customers across almost every market area are seeking an experience. They want to "feel" something from you! And these potential customers are smart! They do their research. They compare you to a myriad of others.

How can you influence their thinking and feelings so that your brand can be recognized as a viable alternative? How can you do this without manipulating people or, worse, misleading them? Let's start with the basics. The working definition of manipulation states:

"Manipulation is to control, coerce or play upon someone by artful, unfair or insidious means - especially to one's own advantage."

To me, lying to someone is tantamount to changing someone's thinking. By being disingenuous or positioning your product or service in such a way that it is misleading or misrepresenting, this is MANIPULATION.

Fortunately, manipulation does have a very close cousin - INFLUENCE. But you must be very careful as the art of "influencing" can often lead to negative manipulation. Look at the definition of influencing:

"To affect, alter or control opinion by indirect or intangible means."

At times, this "cousin" can also exhibit similar patterns that can be misleading. You need to be cautious about your intent.

The key is to be genuine about your product or service and utilize clear techniques. You actually can "influence" someone into a different mindset. Through this type of influence, you can get them to change their mind about a product or service they are currently using and switch over to yours.

On LinkedIn, you see the word "influencer" thrown around like a commodity. Equal to #topvoice and other monikers. An overwhelming majority of the time, I believe these people have nothing but the very best of intentions. They have created personal and professional branding that really resonates with people who follow them and are a part of their network. Their posts provide valuable insight and interesting or entertaining content that many of us learn a lot from.

But make no mistake, this same majority of people are here to grow their businesses. And if I am being transparent, I, too, am here to grow my business -- whether by learning new strategy techniques, coaching ideas, marketing tips, or more. I try to engage often!

The key is that real people of influence, real products or services that influence, don't "manipulate" you into doing anything. Rather, they influence your decision-making in a wide variety of ways. And it truly is an art form because it can be very easy to topple over to the #darkside and try to manipulate people. I hope this article illustrates the clear differences and provides a few tips to get you started.

Let's look at some examples in marketing of what it means to manipulate vs. influence. These are all real examples of differences in messaging I have encountered over the years. See how they appear quite simplistic? In reality, they were old-school and subtle, without much "interrupting."

Comparing the MANIPULATOR with the INFLUENCER:

☻**The Manipulator:** *Negatively compares their products to another, leading with a solution: "Unlike product X, our product does..."*

☻**The Influencer:** *Tells a story – "We hear from customers that they wish product X would do....did you know that our product offers you an alternative that can. . ."*

☻**The Manipulator says:** *"If product X were so good, why do they price it so low....it must not be that great. They have to price it that low to move it."*

☻**The Influencer says:** *"Sometimes we are less expensive, and sometimes a bit more. But we are always competitive, and we strive to provide the best overall value to you."*

☻**The Manipulator says:** *"Don't be fooled by medicine that tastes good. If it tastes bad, that actually means the medicine is working."*

☻**The Influencer says:** *"Sometimes, the most effective medicines don't always have the best taste. Have you tried to take it with food or a beverage?"*

☻**The Manipulator says:** *"Our product does what theirs does but for a lot less money."*

☺**The Influencer says:** *"Oftentimes, our product is very similar to others, and you can obtain the same results without having to spend extra money."*

These examples show subtle differences overall but a VERY different approach. The key thing with manipulation is this: if you ever feel pressured or shamed into taking some kind of action, then you are likely being manipulated. Here is a small example: When you see or hear phrases like *"I only want to speak with people that are truly ready to make drastic changes in their lives; this way, I know you are committed..."* or something similar, this is a type of manipulation. It basically is shaming you or trying to make you feel bad if you don't take the action the person "selling" wants you to take.

A person of influence would modify the phrasing (and hopefully you have also seen this too - I know some amazing coaches have recently linked me in): *"Are you not achieving the results you want? Do you desire to change your life in ways you never imagined? I can help. Join me in my XXXX class, and you will see amazing results, etc. etc., etc. "*Same aggressive message, but no pressure or shame to take an action.

So, how can we all walk the fine line between influencing or manipulating behavior? The following are 3 tips I have found that work well in my boutique consulting firm, TRA Perception Management. My partners and I do our best to implement this strategic approach with our clients. We have found it yields really great and sustainable results!

👁**#1** Be super clear on the #who and #why you are. Or if a product or service, be super clear on "what your product or service is" and "why it can do what it does (and why you created it)." This pushes you to be authentic and genuine. It is hard to manipulate others when you know exactly WHO you are, WHY you are, and WHAT you stand for, etc.

👁#2 Develop multiple ways to #interrupt. If on a personal level, create different ways to interrupt how people think or feel about you. These interruptions help to influence how they perceive you. They can be funny, musical, or literally anything. Don't just have one, though. Sometimes, it takes multiple interruptions to get people to lose a specific opinion or thought of you. With a product or service, develop ways to interrupt how people think or feel about their markets, current products, or services. Over the years, I have found that the best way to intervene in this area is to uncover market opportunities.

👁#3 Develop a way to position your solution by being genuine, outcome-focused, focused, and consistent. Many people get through the first two steps without any issues. Often, I have found that positioning what you have can be a challenge with so many platforms we can use. The key is to be consistent across all platforms (all media, all technology) and brand yourself as the solution provider. You have what people are seeking! And most importantly, you must position yourself very *quickly* after you have interrupted how people think/feel about the product and service they currently use.

Here is a specific example of a client where these principles worked very well. We were able to "influence," not manipulate, an entire market:

The client was a biotech company that competed in the Total Parental Nutrition market in the ICU in Hospitals. This company's product was getting crushed by competitors because it was a lyophilized powder (meaning it required sterile water to mix with it prior to going into an IV). All the other competitors were already in liquid form in small glass vials. Each product cost around the same at the base (except after you mixed in sterile water + nursing time to do this, their product was about 15% higher overall). This Product, "X," was 4th in the marketplace out of 5. How could they possibly compete?

I did the following to help guide this company to a stronger market share and sustainable growth:

I first executed a thorough Perception Analysis. We learned from hospitals, doctors, and nurses that aluminum content in TPN solutions created a dangerous problem, especially for babies in the NICU. Aluminum gets into muscles and bones and slows down development. I had our lyophilized powder analyzed for aluminum content. Guess what? Product X had almost no detectable amounts in the powder form. After the sterile water was added when compared with all the competitors, Product X not only had the lowest amount but was 25 times lower than the next lowest competitor. As you can imagine, this was HUGE.

1) I helped them become super clear on the "who" they were as a company and product. The safest available treatment in this particular TPN therapy. We then focused on their "why" - because TPN therapy is supposed to save lives, not inhibit healing, so I got them excited that this is what they did effectively and safely.

But how do you effectively position this awesome product now without "slamming" competitors directly and trying to manipulate people into using your product?

2) We interrupted the market. We interrupted how physicians, nurses, pharmacists, and hospitals thought about the safety and efficacy of TPN therapy. We interrupted through using thought-provoking education in a variety of formats. We had round table discussions with key opinion leaders (physicians and pharmacy experts in the field) about aluminum content and the dangers it can cause. Clinical evaluations were performed. We had white papers published, testimonial videos made, blogging, and much more. All without ever mentioning a competitor. In fact, the focus was solely on raising awareness for healthcare professionals around the dangers of aluminum content in TPN therapy and how important it was to check the levels of what they currently use so that they can provide the safest TPN possible.

As you can imagine, this issue has become one of the largest and most important topics in hospital ICUs and emergency rooms. We created quite a buzz in a very short period of time (under 6 months).

3) I helped them develop a compelling way to position their solution to what was now a very real problem in the market. The messaging positioned their solution in such a way that it helped Product X grow to almost 80% market share in the 12 months following our "interruption (18 months total)." The message and rebranding were clear, concise, and consistent across all media platforms and selling materials.

Chapter 18
Don't Take It Personally --> Perceptual coaching tips to share with your clients (great for personal coaching or business coaching).

In a recent **PerceptionMakerMoment** video, I shared the importance of not taking ANYTHING personally with regard to critique, criticism, praise, compliments, or any other feedback you receive. It certainly is a provocative way to think about changing behaviors.

As Leaders, our goals should be three-fold when it comes to employee work performance:

✓ **We should create an environment that allows for creativity without fear**

✓ **We should provide a clear path to learning and growing our employee's skill sets**

✓ **We should coach in such a way that we achieve the desired outcomes we want from each of our employees.**

I have had discussions with multiple Life Coaches and read several books written by experts in modifying human behavior through various techniques (NLP, BMI, etc.). I wanted to understand their approach to providing feedback to their clients. There was a clear and common theme that came to light around the performance of their clients. In most cases, their clients were entrepreneurs and people who seemed driven to succeed but somehow had "speed bumps" preventing them from achieving their goals and desired outcomes for their businesses. This theme was around changing behaviors by changing beliefs.

Let's start with companies and their leaders first: The 3 objectives I named above all sound well and good, but in my experience over the past 30 years, although most leaders mean well, very few achieve all three of these objectives. Many don't achieve any of them. In today's day and age, it stands to reason that our customers are searching for an "experience." It makes perfect sense that our employees are seeking the same!

Goals A & B are for another article and/or video. Today, I want to focus on letter C. Take a minute and ask yourself: how do I coach? How do I provide feedback? (this goes for Life Coaches as well). There are multiple formulas for providing feedback:

Classic A) "The Sandwich" often used with younger, less experienced employees >> Starts with a compliment or something positive, moves to the challenge you need to be addressed with their behavior and ends with another compliment or something positive.

Classic B) "Rip off the Band-Aid" often used with employees with significant tenure >> Starts with the issue that needs to be addressed and exactly what will happen if the behavior doesn't change.

Classic C) "What would you do" often used with employees who are strong critical thinkers >>Starts with a story about a hypothetical behavior that needs to be changed and asks the employee how they would handle the issue.

Obviously, these are only three scenarios, and there are many more, but I am guessing you are nodding your head about one approach or another. I am sure you also have others you have heard, seen, or read about, so notice that I am not saying one approach is right or wrong. Why?

It all comes down to the situation, and situational leadership dictates that there is no "best" way for every employee. In fact, we must tweak and modify our approach depending on each individual employee we manage.

But there is one very important thing we can communicate with all our employees: regardless of who they are --> *feedback should not be taken personally!*

Here is another story from Dr. Wayne Dyer about an awesome leader we can relate to. Over 10 years ago, I had the real pleasure of attending a multi-speaker seminar on ways to provide coaching and managing employees. I especially enjoyed the part about providing feedback where Dr. Dyer was one of the keynote speakers. He introduced the concept of "don't take it personally" to the audience. Everyone attending was considered a leader in their organization (Director-level or higher) in our respective companies.

We all came in with solid experience managing others. I can only speak for myself, but this idea was quite new to me. For years, we have been taught (from childhood) that if someone calls us names, is hateful, or we get negative feedback in any way, we shouldn't take it personally. Dr. Dyer said this holds true for **EVERYTHING** positive as well. We shouldn't take any positive feedback personally, either.

To me, this was provocative. It disrupted what I always thought. In his presentation, he focused on the fact that all feedback provided (positive or negative) had only one of two purposes:

You want a behavior to be changed (and sometimes immediately), or
You want a behavior to continue (and even evolve more)

While sitting there, I was thinking to myself – ***he is certainly a master of the obvious***! I didn't expect that he said that the best coaches he has been around made sure that the people they were coaching understood that feedback is simply a tool. It is information you can personally use to gain a behavioral outcome. Any other thinking around this adds complexities that don't need to be there.

If you receive negative feedback, you should take a few minutes and let it soak in. Do your best to understand what behavior(s) you did that gained a negative perception from others. Think about why it was brought to your attention {hint: people want whatever the behavior you are doing to change}. Take another few minutes to be sure you understand "how" you can modify your behavior and write down an action plan. And here comes the most important part – ***DON'T TAKE IT PERSONALLY***. Someone was providing feedback on your actions, not on YOU as a person. So, get over it and make the required changes.

If you receive positive feedback (that "attaboy/girl" pat on the back or even a promotion), you should equally take a few minutes to let it soak in. Do your best to understand what behavior(s) you did that gained this positive perception from others. Consider why they chose to bring it to your attention {hint: they want this behavior to continue}. Take another couple of minutes to be sure you understand "how" you can maintain and continue your behavior and write down an action plan for doing so. And just like the negative feedback, here comes the most important part – ***DON'T TAKE IT PERSONALLY.*** Someone was providing feedback on your actions, NOT on you as a person. So, don't get an ego. Focus on what you can do to continue these great behaviors.

What happens when you clearly communicate that feedback (negative or positive) should not be taken personally? You create an environment where people are not afraid to make mistakes. You have an atmosphere of creativity without fear. Growth and productivity are almost certain to prosper in such an environment. The key is to be consistent. Be clear it is a behavior that you want to be modified, not someone's personality.

How does this relate to Life Coaches? This is part of what we all know to be true about "stinkin' thinkin'." I bet you never thought that "over-basking" in the light of a compliment could be considered "bad" thinking, but it definitely is. Most people get "big heads" because when they are told they are doing something right, they focus on how great they think they are vs. the behavior that someone actually recognized.

I am not a specific Life Coach per se (I focus way more on business and strategy coaching), but it stands to reason that the best way to modify behavior and have the proper influence is to create an environment where people feel safe, supported, and nurtured to success. This is not to say we won't give a "kick in the pants" where needed – but it should always come from a place of wanting a behavior changed and not a personality.

Feedback is an amazing tool and, when used appropriately, will almost always allow for the modifications and/or continuation of behaviors we seek as leaders and coaches.

My challenge to you all is this: When developing the process for providing feedback to your employees or clients, be sure to spend some time on training around communicating that feedback should never be viewed as personal and the exact purpose of why it is used. Don't lose sight of the fact that feedback is a tool to help modify behavior or to gain a continuation of an existing behavior.

Chapter 19
The difference between lateral thought and logical thought.

There are amazing lessons we can all learn from stories and parables. I tried an experiment a few days ago and posted part of a story in my LinkedIn feed. I didn't finish the entire story as I was looking for insights into what others might do. My goal was to see if anyone would come up with a similar solution to what happened in the original story.

To my amazement....NO! Not one person came up with something similar. Several people #overthought their answers, and some people gave quite #simplistic ideas (which is fine, but nothing was innovative). Everyone seemed to continue a "linear" way of thinking vs. a "logical" way of thinking. The term "think outside the box" refers to those who can interrupt their linear thinking to develop different and innovative solutions to a problem or challenge.

Lateral thinking, a term coined by noted author and consultant Edward de Bono, describes a deliberate, systematic process to develop more innovative thinking. In reality, it implements one of the Principles of Perception Management called interruption. By using this interruption principle, whatever situation you are in, by using unconventional thinking techniques you may have never tapped into, you can interrupt the way you and others are thinking and feeling about whatever situation you are in and create a different outcome.

The following short story, also by Edward de Bono, shows a great illustration of this interruption principle in action:

A farmer owed a local loan shark a lot of money. This loan shark was really ugly (inside and out). The farmer had a beautiful young daughter that the loan shark favored.

The loan shark decided he would make a deal and proposed to the farmer that he would waive the debt owed in return for the hand of his beautiful daughter in marriage. Both the farmer and daughter were shocked and disgusted at the proposal.

In any case, the shrewd loan shark wanted to make his proposal "fairer" to the young lady. He said he would put two pebbles into a bag - one black and one white and the daughter would pick one. If she picked a black pebble, she would marry him, and he would forgive all her father's debt. If she picked the white pebble, she did not have to marry him, yet he would still forgive her father's debt. If she decided not to pick a pebble, he would have her father imprisoned for failing to pay off the debt.

With that said, the loan shark picked up two pebbles from the ground, which was full of white and black pebbles, and put them in a bag. However, the young girl's sharp eyes caught the loan shark stuffing two black pebbles into the bag.
As you can imagine, the girl was faced with 3 immediate choices:

1) She could reach into the bag and pull out both pebbles and expose the loan shark for the cheat he was.

2) She could sacrifice herself, choose one pebble, and ensure her father's debt is forgiven.

3) She does nothing - decide not to choose a pebble and allow her father to go to jail.

In my original LinkedIn post, I asked what YOU would do.
As I mentioned at the start of this chapter, the solution calls for implementing the Principles of Perception Management. Specifically, using lateral thinking vs. logical thinking so that you can interrupt the situation.

What do you think the farmer's daughter did? She was such a clever young lady!

She reached into the bag and picked out one pebble. She pulled it out, but before anyone could see what color she picked, she immediately dropped it onto the ground, where it mixed with all the other black and white pebbles.

"Oops. Clumsy me." announced the young girl apologetically.
She then quickly said, "Never mind. The pebble left in the bag will prove which pebble I picked first, so there is no problem." She knew very well the other pebble left in the bag was black. And that way, "proves" the first pebble must have been white. The loan shark did not dare reveal he cheated in the first place and, therefore, had to forgive the debt without getting a bride in return.

As you can see, by using lateral thinking to interrupt the situation, the farmer's daughter quickly changed the outcome! The moral of this story is this: if you change perceptions, you can change your outcomes. So, let's review the "how" behind this lateral thinking process:

The Interruption: The girl dropped the pebble quickly onto the ground with the other white and black pebbles. This caused an immediate *STOP* in how the loan shark and the farmer were thinking about the possible outcome.

New Positioning: The girl immediately positioned the idea that since she dropped one of the pebbles (supposedly, there was only one black and one white), whatever was left inside the bag would show the color of the one she must have dropped. Thus changing the perception that both the loan shark and the farmer had of the situation.

Modified Outcome: A behavior change took place (the loan shark did not want to be exposed, so he modified his actions). The girl did not have to marry the loan shark, and the debt was forgiven -- this apparently was the only outcome the daughter would accept, so she found a way to make it happen.

We are faced with situations, challenges, and problems like this in business and our personal lives every day! I have said it before and will continue to say it repeatedly: If you change perceptions, you change what's possible.

Prologue

I hate goodbyes and endings. I hope that by reading this "how to" guide, you are able to glean some sound ideas about what Perception Management is and how you can implement it in your personal and professional lives. I have some special "thank yous" I want to put out there:

SPECIAL THANKS TO:

- All the original authors for some of my quotes. I hope I did you justice by calling you out by name and using your quotes correctly to illustrate my points.
- My friends and family read the original kooky manuscript and provided directions so I could turn it into an actual book.
- Basically, anyone who has positively influenced me during my life.

If you change perceptions, you really can change what's possible!

About the author:

David Rosenberg is an award-winning marketing strategy leader helping companies turn around under performing products and services or bringing new, innovative products to market. He has strong experience working with businesses of all sizes from start-up to multi-billion dollar bio-pharma, medical device, and large scale manufacturing companies.

Experience matters! With an extensive background in Perception Management (a unique, perceptual approach to strategy), David is known for developing interruptive marketing strategies that achieve great results.

Currently, David is the President & CCO of Woosh Marketing Consultants. Prior to this role, he has held senior leadership positions in sales, marketing, and strategy for companies ranging from start-up to multi-billion dollar corporations. With experience in the Medical field (including Medical Device, Pharma/Biotech, Med Spas, Dentistry), CPG (including skincare, clothing, and giftware), small businesses (including Accounting firms, Law firms, trucking companies, Film & TV), start-ups (including high-tech, new restaurants and more) across multiple markets globally and wearing multiple hats, he is uniquely qualified to help businesses thrive - whatever kind they are.

You can contact David at Woosh Marketing Consultants by visiting www.wooshconsultants.com